Benevolence

Benevolence

A Short Poem Book

LIZETTE KOKKALIS

Benevolence

Copyright © 2019 by Lizette Kokkalis. All rights reserved.

No part of this publication may be reproduced, stored in a retrieval system or transmitted in any way by any means, electronic, mechanical, photocopy, recording or otherwise without the prior permission of the author except as provided by USA copyright law.

The opinions expressed by the author are not necessarily those of URLink Print and Media.

1603 Capitol Ave., Suite 310 Cheyenne, Wyoming USA 82001
1-888-980-6523 | admin@urlinkpublishing.com

URLink Print and Media is committed to excellence in the publishing industry.

Book design copyright © 2019 by URLink Print and Media. All rights reserved.

Published in the United States of America
ISBN 978-1-64367-798-9 (Paperback)
ISBN 978-1-64367-797-2 (Digital)
09.02.19

Contents

Affected 7
Alone Mind 8
Breaking 9
Christmas 10
Dead 11
Empathy 12
Eyes 13
Fire 14
Full Moon 15
Have you? 16
Home 17
In Life 18
In Time 19
Love or Lust? 20
Love 21
Madness 22
Meeting and Leaving 23
Memory 24
Monkey 25
Mother 26
Nature 27
Numb 28
Oh Good Samaritan 29
Our Hearts 30
People 31
Power 32
Rude 33
Skills 34

Steady Eyes 35
The Crow... 36
The Darkness 37
The Dim Light... 38
The Happy Ending... 39
The Lion 40
The Love Wheel 41
The Ocean.. 42
The Road 43
The Ways 44
Tiger 45
Time 46
About the Author.. 47

Affected

Affected by the world, the bad?
Remember there is good too
Think of the light not the dark
Affected by the loss?
Think of it this way, the person is looking at you
Affected by war?
Think of it this way, there are heroes
Yes, you are affected but you are not alone
There will always be someone

Alone Mind

You can fall to pieces
You can fall out of place
Or out of time

You may feel like there is no hope
Like chopped liver
Like darkness in a bad place
You may feel hopeless, but you are not

You may be in a bad state of mind
However,
Your are special to your friends and family
You are wonderful
You are special to the world

Breaking

Are you breaking?
In life we are all breaking
No one is perfect,
No life situation will be
Everyone should believe in something or someone
For that person would not feel alone in this world

Christmas

The snow
The cold air in my bones
The singers down the block
My family next to me singing along
Gifts in bags
Christmas, the best time of the year
My family and I having hot chocolate
A fabulous dinner
We are enjoying the holiday
There may be an argument
Lots of laughter, sharing, carols
Most of all, family always together
That defines Christmas to me

Dead

Are we dead with no soul in this godless world?
Will we go onto the next life?
Laugh so what we are one of the dark
You think not
Well, see you in hell then your blood on my hands
You're crying
Well, wait until I come back

Empathy

Empathy is in you
Empathy is your soul
Keep in mind what is right remember
what is right and what is wrong
You should alway's forgive or your soul way darken
Forgiveness will let your soul free

Eyes

Eyes can cut you with a look
Or they can make you with a look
They are the windows of your soul
A killer has a twisted soul
If the soul is twisted then the soul is bad
A killer is condemned for his sins at the end of his time

fire

Fire is in the hearts of all of us
It may be a good or bad fire
It may break a persons' soul or help their soul
It can take a month, a year, or a lifetime
Be mindful of the fire in your heart

Full Moon

Full moon
The weird one's are out
Legends say
The full moon made men monsters
Because of killings and corpses
The moon has lost some of its power
Still, it can sometimes
Make men monsters on the inside

Have you?

We are human's we make mistakes take it slow
We are not robots
Emotions we were made to love and feel, etc
How do you cope with a mistake take
it slow think before you react?
If you make a mistake it is not the end
the world, it is not a close door
A mistake is what makes you human
and is what makes who you are

Home

Home is a place of solitude, peace, love
Home is where the heart is
Where your family is
Where you can be yourself
The place where you can read
without anyone interrupting
To have peace and quiet
Home is where the heart is

In Life

Life is a blast if you know where to look
The party can be a new page in your
life or it can be a bad one
The new chapter in your life can make you
feel pain like an embarrassment or
It can make you feel full of pride

In time

In time we grow
When we grow things can hurt us
We can overcome it

Feel like you are in deep water
Swim out to the ground
In time you will heal
It may take a long time
But it will happen

If your heart is closed,
open it
If your heart is breaking,
rise from the pain

In time
You have the power in you

Love or Lust?

Is it love or lust when you think you love someone?
You have to let him go at some point
To find out if it is real or not

It may be lust if it is untrue
It will be heartbreaking, but you
must move on with your life
If you don't move on
It will feel like you're drowning
Or like you're burning inside

If it is love
Your heart will let you know

Love

Love is warm
It is not hurtful
It is hurtful when it is not love
because it may be attraction
Trying to get over someone from the
past can be heartbreaking
But moving on can be triumphant

Madness

Madness can control you to make poor choices
Take a deep breath and let the steam out
Let your madness go
Life is too short to be mad at someone

Meeting and Leaving

At the first meeting hearts beat fast and
hands are in the air ready to embrace
Thoughts in your head - Is this right or is this wrong?
Can it work or will it be another heartbreak?
With a look in your eyes comes a light to my soul
Years later we are in a heart shaped coffin

Memory

In memory we think of all things carefully
Our minds can do wrong to us
Our minds can be wrong or right, you are the judge

Be the right judge of your memory
If you are wrong you could hurt someone

Think once, think twice
In the memory
Play it like a video
Over and over
Be the right judge

Monkey

The lovers pen - so you love me
more, but why take my pen?
Oh well, you are like a monkey
You are full of yourself and hate almost everything

You are like a cat, I'm like a dog
The lovers pen has a soul to me
Like my thoughts, they go out with it

I am an empty shell
Run monkey, I'll get it back

Oh… I miss the feeling of my soul pen in my small hands

Mother

Mother is lovely
Mother is mother earth
My world
Reason of living
She is like mother Mary
She is pure

Nature

In our view of nature,
The burning sun comes out
The sun is bright and powerful
It can save us or kill us

In our view of nature,
The water runs
The water is soothing
It is full of life and creatures
It keeps us alive but it can drown us

In our view of nature,
Our surroundings
May be bright and dark
Wet and dry
Nature keep us alive and full of hope

Numb

The numbness in your body
Is it a disease or is it just your mind?
The mind can play tricks and can make
your body feel weak like a piece of
paper
A piece of paper that so easily flies away
Someday someone will catch you from the fall in time

Oh Good Samaritan

Oh good samaritan
So courageous
Good samaritan
Not selfish
Not greedy

Oh good samaritan
It must have been hard
To jump to save a life

Oh good samaritan
You showed not fear
At that time
At that moment
Thank you sweet samaritan

Benevolence

Our Hearts

The days of our lives are numbered
Make every moment count
Do not always think with your mind but with your heart
The heart never lies

People

People come and go
That is life and it is not easy
It will be easy later
It may feel like a sharp pain sometimes
As if you were having a heart attack
Think about the good memories
Not about the bad ones
People may be gone in a second
Make every minute count

Power

Is power all you need? Or is love all you need?
Love and power go hand to hand
Do not overuse them
The heart is weak be careful with your power to the heart
Is power all you need? or is love what you need?
You pick

Rude

So rude to the core
So stubborn to the core
Rude to the fullest
God is on my side
Oh praise the Lord give me strength

Skills

What is your skill in your heart and eyes
Skill can be anything you but you mind too
Skill is it in your reach it may be not
that way but it is alway's believe
Your skill will blossom

Steady Eyes

Steady eyes no smile like me
Steady eyes looking my way
My steady eyes looking your way
We both had no smile for days
Was it fate
With a kiss I thought it might have been
I moved, you had not smile and I did not have one either
We said good bye with steady eyes

The Crow

Crows feet and human hands
Are we beasts or are we humans?
We are unique like all things on earth and in nature
We are prideful in doing the things we please
We are a kingdom of beasts and a kingdom of humans
Some kill, others heal
Some move through life as an outcast
Others live life as King and Queen
Then there's the average Joe
Why is life so hard for some?
Yet, so easy for others?
We might never know

the Darkness

The darkness in this place is all we have
One way ticket to hell will you stay on the ride or not?
I want to stay on the ride
It's the end of my pain
Bye

the Dim Light

The dim light is powerful because it's full of emotions
It is heaven
Heaven is warm and welcoming
Loved ones are in earshot
Far away in the sky
In God's Kingdom you are Home

The Happy Ending

In this life we breath for a happy ending
Will it happen?
Only time will tell and not just time
but with your hard work it do
It does not just happen
Will he or she be your happy ending?
Shall you think with your heart or your mind?
Think with your mind and heart and
then you will get the answer

It may take time
Love is not always smooth
Love can be like war
The relationship can be as smooth
as butter and not fulfilling
Romance can be war and bring us joy
Working it out it is in your hands and in
your lovers hands to the future.

the Lion

In the lions's den the lion is stronger than man
The lion will over power you and crush you to pieces
Men fear him and so do I
Should I run away or become dinner to the lion

The Love Wheel

The love wheel
Can it overcome it all or will it be a battle?
Is it fulfilling and caring?
It can cause conflict if two lovers
personalities are opposite
Will it bring out the good or the bad in the other?
Time will tell

The Ocean

The beautiful ocean is full of life
It has good creatures and bad creatures
The ocean can be calm or can be dangerous
It is unpredictable
The ocean can affect our moods
It is the ocean

the Road

The road is long almost never ending
Will I make it?
I'm always looking to make sure
everything is okay in the end
Weight off my shoulders is power to me
I will always be a survivor

The Ways

The ways of human nature are of hope and disaster
Human nature is like a ying- yang,
one minute happy, then sad
No one knows what's going to happen
One day you are warm in your bed then
the next day you are six feet under

Tiger

The tiger might fear the beast because it has
long claws, sharp teeth, and a big ego
The tiger might eat you alive but do not fear him
I am just pulling your leg
You should fear the tiger if you are
not the beast in the jungle
Get your sword and get your boxing gloves
Here comes the tiger

time

The universe and time
How do they relate?
Is it just a clock with ticking hands?
The sun is the real time
In the old days the old people relaxed
with the sun as their clock__

About the Author

Lizette is a young active woman who has been a book lover since a very young age. At school, she was very attentive and enthusiastic during reading circle time. When she went home, she retold the story or stories of the day to mother and drew pictures about them.

As Lizette started growing, she will make sure to carry a couple of books wherever she went. One of her favorite places to go was the public library or Barnes and Noble bookstore.

She describes her poetry as being inside her soul and in her bones. From her inside, poems come to her heart, then to her mind, eyes, and to the pen to the paper.

Besides her deep affection for reading and writing, Lizette enjoys photography, painting, and ceramics. She is also physically active. She goes to the gymnasium four times a week, swims, and used to be in her school basketball team.

Lizette was born in Queens, New York, on May 15, 1992.

www.ingramcontent.com/pod-product-compliance
Lightning Source LLC
LaVergne TN
LVHW012103070526
838200LV00073BA/3407